SUPERBASE 9
YUMA

SUPERBASE 9

YUMA

The Marines' Mean Machines

George Hall

Published in 1989 by Osprey Publishing
Limited
59 Grosvenor Street, London W1X 9DA

British Library Cataloguing in Publication
Data
Hall, George
    Yuma: the marines' mean machines
    1. United States. Marine Corps,
    Military aircraft
    I. Title   II. Series
    623.74'6'0973

ISBN 0-85045-946-X

Editor Tony Holmes
Designed by Paul Kime
Printed in Hong Kong

Front cover Following a hectic
ACM mission high above the
Arizona desert an Israeli built IAI
Kfir F-21A from VMFT-401 'Snipers'
recovers at MCAS Yuma. Mounted
beneath the delta wing affixed to a
Sidewinder missile rail is an
AIS/ACMI combat sensor pod

Back cover A multi role aircraft at
its best, the AV-8B Harrier II is
an excellent 'dogfighter' as well as a
deadly 'mud mover'. Configured for
both eventualities, this VMA-513
'Flying Nightmares' AV-8B cruises
towards the Yuma weapons range

Title pages 'As the sun sets slowly
in the west. . .' Like most bases
MCAS Yuma retains a link with its
past by displaying several aircraft
as gate guardians. The A-4L
Skyhawk is displayed in VMAT-102
markings, the F-4S Phantom II
represents a VMFAT-101 machine
and the recently positioned AV-8C
Harrier wears VMA-513 'Flying
Nightmares' colours. An MIM-23A
HAWK (homing-all-the-way-killer)
surface-to-air missile battery
completes the display

Right Just prior to taxiing out on a
mission, a pilot from VMFA-323
'Death Rattlers' performs the last of
his preflight checks. The 'Death
Rattlers' have flown the Hornet since
1983 and participated in the El
Dorado Canyon operation against
Libya in 1986 as part of CVW-13,
embarked on the USS *Coral Sea*
(CV-43). Marine Corps F/A-18
drivers now wear a camouflaged
cloth cover over their bone domes,
thus removing another colourful link
with the past

Introduction

Drive east on Interstate 8 out of cool, coastal San Diego—America's biggest navy town—and the geography changes rapidly. After an hour in the mountains, you'll enter the agriculturally rich Imperial Valley. On the left you'll see tactical jets in the pattern over NAS El Centro, including perhaps the Blue Angels, who use the base for their annual training work-ups. Then you're into the merciless American desert, where three-digit temperatures are the norm for most of the year.

Three hours from the coast is the town of Yuma, Arizona, site of the Old West's grimmest territorial prison and frequently the hottest spot in the entire US. The weather may be rough on joggers, but it's a paradise for military aviation; 340 days per year with perfect flying conditions and close proximity to 1.5 million acres of bombing and manoeuvre ranges. That's an area bigger than the state of New Jersey.

In Yuma the US Marine Corps is operating its largest western air base, with military take-offs and landings creeping steadily upward toward 150,000 per year. The runways hum with jet activity from pre-dawn until well after dark. Over 100 Navy and Marine Corps units with almost 1000 aircraft deploy to Yuma each year to take advantage of the magnificent flying conditions and the sophisticated, electronically monitored ranges.

Strictly a training base before 1986, MCAS Yuma is now transitioning to a tactical air station. When this process is complete in 1991, the base will be home to four squadrons of AV-8B Harrier IIs. For a while longer, two squadrons of ageing, but still capable, A-4M Skyhawk light bombers will share the runways with the Harriers. The Marine Corps' west-coast replacement air group (RAG) squadron, VMFAT-101 out of MCAS El Toro, maintains a full-time det at Yuma, as does the Navy Fighter Weapons School, TOP GUN. Many TOP GUN instructional hops originate out of NAS Miramar in San Diego, utilize the Yuma ranges, and then land at Yuma to debrief and prepare for the next mission.

But the resident units are only a part of the story of Superbase Yuma. The flightline is always swelled with units in on 'det', or temporary detachment, for training in the crystalline Arizona skies. Marine helicopters, from the small, flitting AH-1 Cobras to the lumbering CH-53E Super Stallions, do their work-ups regularly at Yuma. Helicopter performance is painfully affected by heat, and a helo that can fly and fight in the Yuma cauldron can do it anywhere. Twice a year the Marine Air Weapons and Tactics School, based at Yuma and known throughout the Corps as 'MAWTS-1', mounts huge flying exercises utilizing all of the Marine air assets and a good sampling of guest participants from the other branches.

It would be hard to name a US Marine or Navy base that can beat Yuma for sheer quantity and variety of day-to-day flight operations. Of course, like all active-duty flying stations in the US, MCAS Yuma is closed to casual visitors, and complex permissions are necessary for anything resembling flightline access. But unlike many bases, Yuma shares its runways with the civilian airport across the field, and there are many excellent vantage points beyond the runways where observers can watch the cream of modern Naval and Marine Corps aviation in action.

But we're 'cleared hot' for flightline photography, thanks to Lt Mary Baldwin USMC and her public affairs staff at Yuma; we will also be making several photo hops over the ranges in the latest Marine tactical aircraft. Let's lather on the sunscreen and find out what makes MCAS Yuma tick.

Contents

Lion of the desert

A rare beast! One of 13 Israeli Aircraft Industries (IAI) F-21A Kfirs attached to Marine Fighter Training Squadron 401 'Snipers' at MCAS Yuma taxies in after a 'photo shoot' with a difference. Mounted on the centreline pylon is the author's camera pod which was developed especially for air-to-air photography

Above Protection is the name of the game at Yuma where temperatures are often above 110°F. A series of shade sheds was built on the flightline to provide accommodation for the Kfirs, and offer some respite from the scorching sun for the Israeli Aircraft Services maintainers. The Kfir is notorious for leaking fluid, as the stained concrete beneath the aircraft proves

Above The Kfirs arrived at MCAS Yuma in June 1987 and were originally to be leased from the Israeli government for four years. However, these aircraft were due to be returned to the Middle East in October 1989, after which they will be replaced by ex-Navy F-5Es. This aircraft has a pair of Sidewinder rails mounted under each wing and the author's camera pod affixed to the centreline pylon

Above The F-21s are painted in standard *Heyl Ha'Avir* desert and air superiority colours. The mixture of colours worn on the Kfirs has worked well with VMFT-401 as some aircraft blend in with the desert landscape while others are 'lost' against the hazy skyline

Right The Kfir is a rapid mover when it comes to leaving terra firma for the heavens above. Wickedly overpowered, the aircraft mounts a Bet-Shemesh licence-built General Electric J79-GE-17 turbojet squeezed into the fuselage. The J79 produces 18,750 lb of thrust on full afterburner, giving the light Kfir a large thrust-to-weight advantage over most of its rivals. Moments after leaving Yuma the pilot begins to retract his undercarriage and commence the rapid climb to mission height. The aircraft has a remarkable climb rate of 47,250 feet a minute with afterburner selected from low level

The near lunar landscape below forms an impressive backdrop for two VMFT-401 Kfirs. Basically a Mirage 5 powered by an F-4 Phantom II engine, the IAI Kfir is still in frontline service with the Israelis, who operate over 200, and Ecuador, which has a squadron of 12. These photos were taken with the camera pod mounted beneath another Kfir

Left Not only does the Kfir motivate on take-off but its recovery speed over the ramp is also rather impressive. As with the Mirage III, the Kfir deploys a large braking parachute once it has touched down. The canards mounted just behind the air intakes improve the overall combat manoeuvrability of the aircraft, as do the small strakes fitted to the Kfir's nose

Above Mission completed, a Kfir returns to base. Attached to each of the Sidewinder rails is an Aircraft Instrumentation Systems (AIS) pod, alternatively designated an Air Combat Manoeuvring (ACMI) pod. Essentially a high tech signals emitter, the AIS/ACMI pod relays altitude, speed and bearing details to the Tactical Air Combat Training System (TACTS) computer back at Yuma

17

Above Adversary and aggressor squadrons have always embraced the ethos of the Soviet fighter pilot to create a camaraderie unique to these élite units. If anything, VMFT-401 go one step further by actually combining the silhouette of their unusual mount with the official Red Army sniper's badge

Right 'Sniper' country is Soviet country! VMFT-401's ready room is also decorated with a definite communistic flavour, the slogan on the wall reading 'Offence is the key to Victory'. Here comrades get the 'gouge' before commencing aerial duels with the enemy

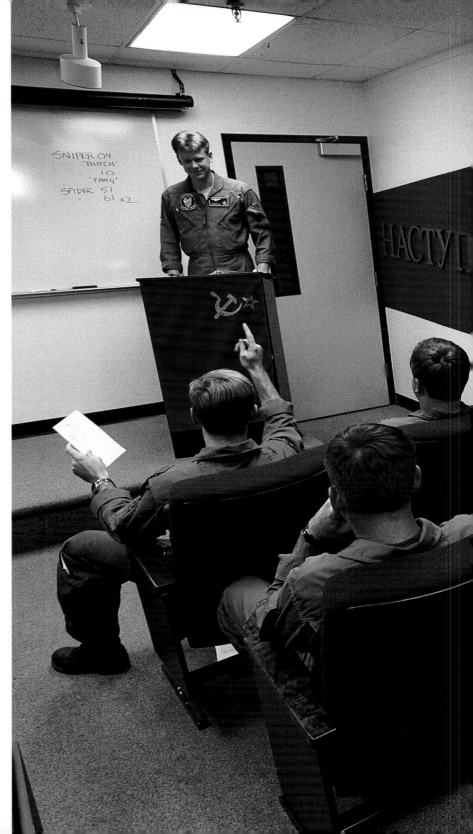

Left The Kfir presents a small head-on area to its opponent making it difficult to see at a distance. The canards fitted to the aircraft can be seen in this view, as well as the pronounced upward tapering of the delta wing. Besides the AIS/ACMI pods mounted on each pylon, a small external tank is fitted to the aircraft's centreline. The drum near the Kfir's left undercarriage leg is positioned under the tail of the aircraft while it is parked to catch some of the fluids which leak from the engine at an alarming rate

Above The cockpit of the Kfir is a tight fit for the average Marine Corps driver. Essentially an aircraft designed in the early 1950s, the Kfir has a definite lack of rearward vision. The small stencil beneath the cockpit is the canopy opening warning

Left FOD ingestion? The Kfirs
are maintained by a mixed
Israeli/American civilian workforce
attached to Israeli Aircraft Services,
a subsidiary of IAI. The leasing of
the actual aircraft cost the US
government nothing but all running
costs incurred were paid for by
them

Above The unusual combination of
the red star and the USMC emblem
is worn with pride on all VMFT-401
machines

Above Kfir is the Hebrew word for Cub Lion, and like Dassault-Breguet, IAI usually decorate the noses of their aircraft with the type's name

Right An impressive head-on view of a Kfir which has just returned from an ACM sortie. The various air scoops mounted on the spine of the aircraft were added to help keep the J79 engine, and various powerplant auxiliary units, cool during flight. The 13 aircraft leased to the USMC are Kfir C-1s, 27 of which were built from 1976 onward. The principal model operated by Israel and Ecuador is the upgraded C-2 version which has a slightly more powerful engine and larger auxiliary canards. Most Kfirs in service with the *Heyl Ha'Avir* have been progressively converted to C-7 standards incorporating a more powerful version of the J79, two additional wing hardpoints, a new hands on throttle and stick (HOTAS) installation and improved avionics into the standard Kfir C-2 airframe. Twelve Kfir C-1s were also leased to the US Navy as F-21As between 1985 and 1988. These aircraft were operated by VF-43 based at NAS Oceana, Virginia

Above A prized possession! The 'Snipers' are the only dedicated fighter
adversary squadron in the Corps and a posting to this élite band is highly
sought after. The conversion training onto the Kfir was a mixed US/Israeli
affair for the potential pilots. Initially they worked up with VF-43 and then
spent a week in Tel Aviv before finally returning to NAS Oceana to complete
their training

Above Another prized possession! The head of the Israeli maintenance staff snagged this 'hot' licence plate soon after the Kfirs arrived at Yuma

Marine heavy metal

The main muscle of Marine Air Group (MAG) 13. The McDonnell Douglas AV-8B Harrier II is steadily becoming the most predominant type of aircraft based at MCAS Yuma, a position jointly held for many years by two other classic McDonnell Douglas designs; the A-4 Skyhawk and F-4 Phantom II. Fully bombed up with four 500 lb Mk 82 'iron' bombs, this AV-8B belongs to VMA-513 'Flying Nightmares', the first Third Marine Aircraft Wing (MAW) squadron to transition onto the Harrier II

Above The heat haze rising from the scorching runway mixes with the vectored thrust from the AV-8B's Rolls-Royce Pegasus turbofan. Harrier IIs rarely recover at MCAS Yuma in this fashion, preferring to approach the runway like any 'normal' combat aircraft. The pilot appears to be glancing over at the Yuma International Airport situated across the field from the air station

Above On first appearances this AV-8B looks just like any other Harrier II based at Yuma. However, all MAG-13 AV-8s wear a two-letter tailcode beginning with W, and this aircraft is coded XE. This AV-8B actually belongs to VX-5 'Vampires', one of the Navy/Marine Corps special test squadrons, based at the China Lake Naval Weapons Center (NWC) in California. All new combat types are thoroughly tested by the 'Vampires', a task shared on the west coast by sister squadron VX-4 'Evaluators', before they are cleared for frontline service. NWC China Lake is only a short distance away from the live ranges at MCAS Yuma, especially when you are flying a Harrier II at Mach 0.8!

Above The 'jungle' camouflage of the AV-8B isn't quite suited to the barren surrounds of MCAS Yuma, but then Arizona is probably the last place that the aircraft would expect to see combat. Toting a pair of AIM-9 Limas and four 500 lb Mk 82 'iron' bombs under its wings, this VMA-513 Harrier II is on its way to the weapons range. The 'double nuts' (00) modex on the nose denotes that this particular aircraft is the CO's mount

Above The visibility for the pilot in the AV-8B is superb, his eye-level having been raised ten inches compared with the AV-8A. McDonnell Douglas quotes vision angles as 17 degrees over the nose and 58 over the aircraft's sides. For successful 'down in the weeds' flying these figures are vital

Above The successful rebirth of the 1960s Harrier into a truly world class combat aircraft of the 1980s and 90s is due in no small part to the highly efficient supercritical wing developed by McDonnell Douglas. Constructed almost entirely of graphite/epoxy composite material, the overall weight saving of the wing structure is roughly 330 lb compared to a conventional wing. Leading-edge wing-root extensions (LERX) can also be seen in this impressive head-on view of a VMA-513 Harrier II. The extensions were added to the AV-8B by McDonnell Douglas after the Royal Air Force requested their inclusion during the redesigning of the AV-8A

Opposite above The overall shape of the Harrier II is still very similar to the original Hawker design. Two of the major evolutionary changes built into the AV-8B can be seen in this photo; the extra outboard wing hardpoints and repositioned outriggers

Opposite below The pilots of the Marine Corps are just like any other military aviators when it comes to recovery back at base after a sortie; the tighter the pitch out, the better the pilot. Wing vortices stain the vivid blue Arizona sky as an AV-8B driver 'struts his stuff' in a five to six G turn

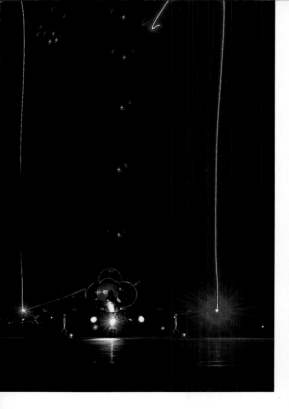

Above Shades of 'Close Encounters of the Third Kind'. A Harrier II performs what it does best during a night recovery

Right The setting sun picks out important details on this AV-8B. The MDC (miniature detonating cord) pattern within the bubble hood breaks the canopy into small fragments to enable the pilot to eject quickly and safely. The angled mounts on the instrument coaming form an essential part of the Smiths Industries SU-128/A HUD (head-up display). Just forward of the windshield is the yaw vane indicator, a vital piece of equipment for the Harrier II pilot while in the hovering position. Finally, the small blade antenna just in front of the yaw vane indicator is the upper IFF (Identification friend or foe) interrogator

Left Operating on the flightline at Yuma becomes a little more bearable after the sun has set. A crew chief discusses the forthcoming mission with his pilot. Besides a Sidewinder under each wing, this VMA-513 machine also carries 12 25 lb blue practice bombs on four triple ejector racks (TERs)

Above The day's flying over, a groundcrewman attaches the protective cover back onto the Hughes Angle Rate Bombing Sensor (ARBS) mounted in the nose of the AV-8B. The ARBS is a television/laser-tracker specially developed for the Harrier II and is linked to the aircraft's mission computer

VMA-513's association with the Harrier goes back some 18 years to April 1971 when the 'Flying Nightmares' became the first combat jet VTOL squadron in the history of US military aviation. The squadron traded in their war-weary F-4B Phantom IIs after returning from a tour of Vietnam in late 1970, and reformed on the much smaller AV-8A at MCAS Beaufort, South Carolina. Over the years the 'Flying Nightmares' deployed regularly with the Harrier on WestPac cruises, adding muscle to US Navy/Marine amphibious groups. The last of these deployments took place in 1986 when VMA-513 sent Det A, equipped with AV-8Cs, to sea with the USS *Tarawa* (LHA-1). In 1987, after transitioning onto the AV-8B, the squadron went to sea with their new mounts for the first time on board the USS *Belleau Wood* (LHA-4)

Left Hot and heavy work for VMA-513 armourers. These 500 lb Mk 82 'iron' bombs have the standard free-fall fins fitted to them. If the AV-8B was configured to carry only this particular weapon, a total of 16 Mk 82s could be slung under the aircraft

Above A genuine 'Flying Nightmare'! VMA-513's executive officer, Major T J Cuny

Fighter/Attack Eighteen

The 'sharp edge' of Marine Corps muscle, the McDonnell Douglas F/A-18A. Carrying a typical war load for a 'leather neck' Hornet of eight bombs and two Sidewinders, this aircraft from VMFA-314 'Black Knights' cruises towards the strike area. Based at MCAS El Toro, California, and one of three F/A-18 squadrons which form part of MAG-11, the 'Black Knights' regularly deploy to MCAS Yuma to take advantage of the 'smart' range strewn across many miles of desert

Left Lead 'Black Knight' pulls in towards the camera over a less than hospitable landscape

Above The F/A-18 is a true all-rounder, its ability to perform as a fighter being matched totally by its prowess as a strike platform. The agility needed to perform both of these roles effectively comes from a soundly designed wing, the product of Northrop's design bureau headed by Lee Begin Jr. Of trapezoidal planform, and incorporating variable camber, the wing is supplanted by substantial leading edge extensions (LEXs) which protrude forward to the cockpit. The LEXs cause strong air flow vortices over the wing allowing the pilot to maintain controlled flight at extreme angles of attack, and generally increasing the wing's maximum lift. High Mach buffet is also limited by the LEX

Above 'Smile'. The pilot looks intently at the author's camera. As far as
F/A-18's go, the overall tactical paint scheme (TPS) on this particular aircraft
is in surprisingly good condition

Above Pilot and machine in perfect harmony with each other. With 'showtime' soon to commence, this 'Black Knight' prepares to dive down into tumbleweed country

Above Mounted inboard from the wing leading edges are two wedge-like vertical surfaces which are being progressively retrofitted to all Hornets. These rather ugly excrescences have been added to the F/A-18 to disturb the channelled airflow which washes over the LEXs and buffets the twin tails violently. Stressed fins and tail 'flutter' have been the Hornet's structural Achilles' heel throughout its brief service career, McDonnell Douglas having already 'beefed-up' the fin-to-fuselage attachment points at considerable cost to the company

Right The 'Black Knights' have the distinction of being the first frontline unit operational on the F/A-18, transitioning onto the aircraft commencing August 1982

Above Resembling a miniaturized forward looking infra-red receiver pod mounted on the wing pylon, this small device is in fact the author's camera pod. Painted up in full TPS colours, the pod is attached to a VMFAT-101 'Sharpshooters' F/A-18. The 'Sharpshooters' have only recently transitioned onto the Hornet from the F-4S Phantom II, a change which coincided with them moving from MCAS Yuma to MCAS El Toro

Right 'Let the games begin!' An F/A-18 driver plays follow-my-leader with four of his squadron buddies

An impressive landscape complements an impressive formation. Ironically, the Kfirs will be acting as enemy MiG-21s and 23s in the battle which is soon to commence, types which they were developed to shoot down. All four aircraft have an AIS/ACMI pod mounted under each wingtip

Above Along with fellow El Toro residents VMFA-323 'Death Rattlers', VMFA-314 saw action in 1986 when the squadron swapped coasts and cruised with CVW-13 on board USS *Coral Sea* (CV-43). Together with VFA-131 'Wildcats' and VFA-132 'Privateers', the two USMC squadrons provided MiGCAP for the Sixth Fleet's A-6s and A-7s, as well as flying anti-radar missions, during the El Dorado Canyon operation

Above Devoid of all external stores, bar two wingtip mounted AIM-9Ls, a 'Grey Ghost' goes looking for trouble. Like all other Marine Corps F/A-18 units, VMFA-531 were long-term F-4 'Phanatics' before updating to the latest St Louis rocket in the summer of 1983. In this configuration the aircraft would be more than a handful for any 'bogeys' the pilot might come across

Above left With his strobe light flashing, a 'Grey Ghost' guides his Hornet back to Yuma, chasing the setting sun as he goes

Above right The big 'bat turn' is a speciality of F/A-18 drivers, and an effective manoeuvre against less nimble opponents like adversary F-5Es and F-21 Kfirs. Although a manoeuvre like this bleeds the aircraft of speed the reheat available to the pilot with the twin General Electric F404-GE-400 turbofans soon makes up the deficit

Right Soon Yuma will be far away as two Hornet pilots retract their gear and disappear into the night

Above The faces behind the 'Knights'. Maintenance man-hours per flight for the F/A-18 are roughly 15 to 16 compared to 45 to 50 with its predecessor, the Phantom II. No wonder they are all smiling!

Right This well used F/A-18B belongs to the Marine Corps' fighter-attack training unit, VMFAT-101 'Sharpshooters'. Although now based at El Toro, the squadron still spend roughly 50 per cent of their time utilizing the facilities and weapons range at Yuma. Initial training on the Hornet is still predominantly carried out by VFA-125 'Rough Raiders', the Navy's replacement air group (RAG) unit at NAS Lemoore, but VMFAT-101 is steadily taking over this role for would-be USMC Hornet drivers. Transitioning onto the F/A-18 usually takes about six months

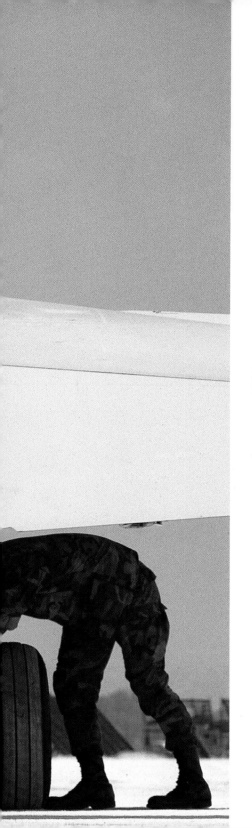

Left The final checks are made on a VMFA-314 Hornet. The heat on the flightline at MCAS Yuma is oppressive to say the least but that doesn't put the groundcrew off the task at hand

Above The 'Black Knights' of VMFA-314. All four pilots have camouflaged cloth covers fitted to their 'bone domes'

Left Flying the flag for the naval side of F/A-18 operations, a brand new VFA-82 'Marauders' machine recovers at MCAS Yuma. The 'Marauders' only recently stood up as a VFA squadron at NAS Cecil Field, Florida, after trading in their A-7E Corsair IIs for factory fresh F/A-18Cs. Visually, the 'C' model can be distinguished from the 'A' by the series of small white blisters which now adorn the nose and spine of the aircraft. These house new airborne self-protection jammers. Other changes to the Hornet include compatibility with the new AIM-132 AMRAAM missile and infra-red imaging AGM-65D Maverick air-to-ground missile, an improved mission computer with more speed and memory, a flight incident monitoring and recording system, new ejection seat and provisions for reconnaissance equipment. Over 700 'C' and 'D' model Hornets are due to be built for the Navy and Marine Corps

Above A long way from home. Another east coast F/A-18 squadron which visited MCAS Yuma late in 1988 was VFA-131 'Wildcats'. Unlike the 'Marauders', the boys from VFA-131 are still equipped with Alpha model Hornets, a type they have flown since October 1983. The 'Wildcats' were the first AirLant (US Navy Air Wing Atlantic) attack squadron to receive the F/A-18. Usually assigned to CVW-13, along with sister squadrons VFA-136 'Knight Hawks' and VFA-137 'Kestrels', the 'Wildcats' were sent on the post-SLEP (service life extension programme) cruise around Cape Horn with the USS *Independence* (CV-62). The '*Indi*' changed home ports during the cruise and now sails out of San Diego, California. VFA-131's usual carrier, the venerable USS *Coral Sea* (CV-43), is currently in Norfolk Naval Yard, Virginia, undergoing a SLEP

Yuma scooter

Besides the Marine Corps A-4M Skyhawks which call MCAS Yuma home, regular visitors to the base are Navy Fighter Weapons School (NFWS) A-4F adversary aircraft. Supplementing VMFT-401's Kfirs, the Navy A-4s provide dissimilar air-combat training not only for the AV-8Bs and F/A-18s of the Marine Corps, but for the 'Snipers' themselves. Unusually for the NFWS both of these Skyhawks are painted in identical schemes. An AIS/ACMI pod is also mounted on the centreline of each A-4

Above Just another A-4F you might think. In fact this particular aircraft, BuNo 152101, was the last 'E' model Skyhawk ever built, and was modified on the production line by McDonnell Douglas engineers in order to serve as the prototype A-4F. It made its first flight on 31 August 1966 and was followed down the El Segundo production line by a further 146 'F' model Skyhawks. I wonder if Captain 'Tex' Allen, currently 152101's pilot, knows the significance of his mount, the 'granddaddy' of all A-4Fs

Right The pilot quickly rotates his undercarriage gear away and points the nose of his A-4 into the wild blue. Slung under the fuselage, mounted on a Sidewinder rail, is the all-important AIS/ACMI pod

Above Not the sort of terrain you would want to get 'bingo' fuel state over!
Wearing a rich tan, chocolate brown and dark green wraparound scheme,
an A-4E from the NFWS, based at NAS Miramar, banks over rugged country
not too far from Yuma

Above Although equipped with aircraft from another generation, the two A-4M squadrons based at Yuma form an integral part of the strike team that is MAG-13. VMA-211 'Wake Island Avengers' are probably the most experienced Skyhawk operators in the world, having received their first A-4As in September 1957! Over the following 32 years the 'Avengers' have flown the Bravo, Charlie, Echo and, since the late 1970s, Mike model A-4s.

Slightly less experienced than VMA-211 on the Skyhawk was fellow Yuma based outfit VMA-311 'Tomcats'. The squadron was issued with A-4Bs in 1958 and followed the 'Avengers' through the family of Skyhawk models. The 'Tomcats' finally bade farewell to the aircraft that had so faithfully served them for thirty years half-way through 1988 when their annual deployment to MCAS Iwakuni, Japan, ended. They relinquished their A-4Ms to fellow Yuma residents VMA-214 'Blacksheep' and returned to Arizona to begin the transition onto the AV-8B

Left The single triple ejector rack (TER) mounted under the wing of this VMA-211 A-4M has been configured to carry six small 25 lb practice bombs, their absence denoting the successful completion of another sortie over the live ranges at Yuma. Along with VMA-214, the 'Avengers' are soon to pass their Mike model A-4s onto various Corps reserve squadrons still equipped with Echo and Foxtrot versions of the Skyhawk

Above One A-4 that will always remain at MCAS Yuma long after the whine of the last Pratt & Whitney J52 turbojet has been swallowed up by the vast Arizona desert, is this mounted tribute to VMAT-102. This particular Skyhawk is one of 100 A-4Cs brought up to A-4F standard during the early 1970s. Designated the A-4L, the aircraft received updated avionics and control systems, but retained the old J65 engine. The Limas served faithfully for many years with the Navy and Marine Corps reserve units until eventually being replaced by A-7A Corsair IIs and Mike model Skyhawks in the mid 1970s

'The duellists'

State of the art adversary. A quantum leap in the services available to fleet fighter squadrons has been achieved since the Navy received its 26 hot F-16Ns. Regularly 'on the road' with their aircraft, these three examples are part of the twelve flown by the Naval Fighter Weapons School. All the maintenance carried out on the F-16 is performed by technicians from General Dynamics, the aircraft's manufacturer. Framed by the radarless nose of a TF-16, one of only two in the squadron, a brace of F-16Ns bake in the Arizona sun on the Yuma flightline

Above The RIO peers over his shoulder as the pilot retracts the gear and leaves Yuma on yet another ACM sortie. Unusually for an adversary aircraft, this TF-16 has an external fuel tank mounted on its centreline pylon

Opposite above The F-14 Tomcat is a rare visitor to MCAS Yuma at the best of times and the fact that these two belong to squadrons based on the other side of the country makes this photo even more noteworthy. Calling NAS Oceana, Virginia, home these two F-14As belong to VF-33 'Starfighters' and VF-74 'Be-devilers'

Opposite below Using full phase five afterburner on take-off, a glossy Tomcat from VF-74 leaves Yuma on a sortie that will see the 'Be-devilers' pitted against a mixed force of F-16Ns and A-4Fs high above the desert. Assigned to Air Wing (CVW) 17, VF-74 usually deploy with the Sixth Fleet on board USS *Saratoga* (CV-60)

Above Fully optimized for an ACM sortie, the pilot tucks up his gear and keeps the wick fully turned up. Mounted on the wing shoulder pylon is an AIS/ACMI pod and a finless infra-red homing Sidewinder missile. Formerly nicknamed the 'Tarsiers', the 'Starfighters' are assigned to CVW-1 and regularly cruise on board the USS *America* (CV-66) with sister squadron VF-102 'Diamondbacks'

Right Framed by the tail of a Yuma based AV-8B, one of the two visiting F-14s launches at dusk on a night mission

Killer punch

Left The heavy all-weather punch of Marine Corps aviation is provided by five attack squadrons equipped with the A-6E TRAM Intruder. Regularly seen at Yuma, where they come to sharpen up their low-level interdiction capabilities, Marine Intruders are based at MCAS El Toro, California, and MCAS Cherry Point, North Carolina, with one squadron sent on a 12 month forward deployment to MCAS Iwakuni with the 1st MAW and MAG-12. Seen at an altitude seldom reached by all-weather attack squadrons while at Yuma, this A-6E TRAM belongs to VMA(AW)-242 'Bats'. The squadron is now once more El Toro based after finishing its stint at Iwakuni and being replaced by VMA(AW)-332 'Polkadots' in June 1988

Below The huge slab wing, and all the surface excrescences, can be seen in this close-up view of the A-6 as the pilot edges his aircraft in towards the author's camera. The leading edge slats are slightly deployed to help the aircraft formate with the 'photo ship', a KC-130F Hercules tanker. This 'Bat' is carrying only a moderate bomb load of eight 500 lb Mk 82 'iron' bombs mounted on a pair of TERs

Pitch out and dive to mission height. The A-6 driver will drop down several thousand feet and begin his run in to the target at virtually tumbleweed height, using the rugged ranges below to mask his attack route into and out of the drop zone from 'enemy' radar. The Target Recognition and Attack Multisensor (TRAM) turret under the nose looks as if it has only just been fitted to this aircraft, the non-standard white fairing around the pod being most unusual. The 'Bats' have flown the Intruder longer than any other Marine Corps unit, taking delivery of their first A-6A at NAS Oceana in mid 1964. Two and a half years later VMA(AW)-242 forward deployed to Da Nang, thus becoming the first Marine Intruder squadron to see combat in Vietnam

One aircraft destined never to see service with the Marine Corps was the chunky Vought A-7 Corsair II. This particular A-7E belongs to the Naval Strike Weapons Center (NSWC), commonly referred to as 'Strike U', at NAS Fallon, Nevada. Along with testing the effectiveness of the ranges at their own base, the highly experienced crews from the NSWC often transit down to Arizona and help the Marines improve their training syllabus

Marking time

An aircraft that needs no introduction. The classic F-4 Phantom II has long been associated with MCAS Yuma; the Marine Corps training squadron VMFAT-101 'Sharpshooters' being based here for over 25 years before they transitioned onto the F/A-18 and moved to El Toro last year. Now, after providing the Marine Corps with over a quarter of a century of sterling service, the 'Phabulous Phantom' is steadily being retired from both frontline and reserve squadrons. Based at Dallas Airport, Texas, this F-4S belongs to VMFA-112 'Wolf Pack', one of three reserve units still plying the skies with the weary warbird

Overleaf A sight never to be repeated. Two 'Sharpshooters' formate over the rugged terrain which surrounds their former base. Being the solitary F-4 training unit in the Corps, VMFAT-101 was responsible for training a countless number of Phantom II drivers and RIOs, many of whom saw extensive combat over the steamy jungles of Vietnam. These two aircraft are 'S' model Phantom IIs, the last to serve with the 'Sharpshooters'

Left With the author's camera pod attached to the starboard wing pylon of an A-4 Skyhawk, the 'scooter' driver formates with the glowing tailpipes of a Marine F-4S at dusk

Above Leaving the familiar dirty black General Electric J79 signature behind it, an RF-4C Phantom II from VMFP-3 'Specters' or 'Eyes of the Corps' comes in on finals to Yuma. Based at El Toro, this unit is the only dedicated photo reconnaissance squadron in the Corps, and a veteran Phantom II outfit to boot!

Lockheed tanker

Above Just like every C-130 Hercules operated around the globe, the
Lockheed transport is an essential workhorse, in this case of the Marine
Corps. As far back as 1960, the first of 46 KC-130Fs ordered by the Corps
was delivered, configured in the assault transport/aerial refueller roles.
Quenching the thirst of two VMFA-531 'Grey Ghost' F/A-18s, this KC-130R
belongs to El Toro based VMGR-352

Above Cruising serenely above the stratocumulus, KC-130F '812' was
originally built for the Marines in the early 1960s. The drogue refuelling pod
is clearly visible under the starboard wing. This Hercules wears the colours
of the recently disbanded VMGR-152, a squadron which spent most of its time
at MCAS Futenma, on the Japanese island of Okinawa, supporting aircraft of
the 1st MAW

Above The two Marine Corps heavy lifters join forces over Yuma as a pair of CH-53Es take it in turns to plug into a KC-130F from VMGR-351. The skill level of a KC-130 pilot has to be extremely high because the variety of aircraft refuelled, and the different cruising speeds associated with each type, dictate that the Hercules tanker must be flown with precision. In this case the huge trailing edge flaps are deployed slightly to allow the Hercules to cruise with the Super Stallions safely

Right Displaying the new trend in KC-130 markings, this 'R' model from VMGR-352 is painted up in the tactical 'ghost' scheme. The boys from VMGR-352 fly in and out of Yuma on a daily basis carrying supplies and parts to and from El Toro. One of the distinguishing features of the Romeo model Hercules is the two extra fuel tanks fitted externally between the Allison T56-A-15 turboprops. The KC-130Rs are virtually brand new and, along with the older Echo models, are having a special countermeasures system developed for them by Lockheed. Called SATIN (Survivability Augmentation for Transport Aircraft-Now!), the programme will see the AN/APR-39(V)1 radar warning receiver, AN/AAR-43 missile detector system and the AN/ALE-39 chaff and flare dispensing kit fitted to the Hercules. USAF C-130s are also currently being modified with SATIN

Transient transports

Left Although not frequenting MCAS Yuma quite as much as the ubiquitous KC-130s, Military Airlift Command (MAC) C-141B Starlifters occasionally call in to the base to bring in troops for manoeuvres or outsize loads which are maybe too bulky for the Hercules. Wearing the now standard Europe One camouflage scheme, this Starlifter is attached to the 63rd Military Air Wing at Norton Air Force Base, California

Below Life at the opposite end of the transport aircraft scale! Wearing the extremely stylish Marine Corps gold and maroon cheatline down the fuselage, the MCAS Yuma Base Flight Beech UC-12 is refuelled, rather unusually, by one of its crew. Although BuNo 161200 wears the UC-12B designation all Marine Corps and Navy Super King Airs have recently been modified to 'M' standard with different cockpit instruments, lighting and voice communications

Above Civilian airliners, chartered by the forces to move troops around more economically, are a regular sight at US bases all over the world. This veteran Boeing 707 is operated by the imaginatively named Skyworld, just one of several small charter firms which rely upon contracts from the military to remain in business

Above A rather unfortunately named Air America Lockheed L-1011 TriStar taxies in at Yuma. The name Air America was chosen by the CIA for their pseudo-airline which operated heavily in South-east Asia during the Vietnamese conflict. The current Air America has no links with its forebear, being employed on military charter work

Aspects of MCAS Yuma

Left The flatness of the land immediately surrounding the air station can be appreciated from this panoramic view of the flightline and associated buildings taken from the Yuma control tower in the late afternoon. The township of Yuma is to the right of the photo

Below Visiting Navy F-14s and F/A-18s dominate this view of the Yuma tower and the impressive mountain ranges which rise out of the desert to the north-west of the base

Left The working space inside the Yuma tower is not huge, but the civilian and military personnnel who occupy it believe it is adequate. At least it is air-conditioned, unlike the vast open space below! Being a joint civil/military facility, diligence is the watchword for both the air traffic controllers and the pilots when in the Yuma pattern

Above Marine controllers hard at work in the air traffic control centre, housed in the base of the Yuma tower. The crowded flight schedule for sorties in and out of the weapons range and regular domestic flights to other states and Mexico combine to make the controllers' day a busy one

105

Left Seen here at their California home of MCAS Camp Pendleton, groundcrewmen from VMO-2 work on an OV-10A Bronco. The Broncos from this squadron regularly deploy to Yuma to provide combat FAC (forward air control) for elements of the 3rd MAW utilizing the facilities at the base

Below An essential piece of equipment at any base is the brutish Chevy four wheel drive truck. This one belongs to Yuma Air Operations, hence the pair of blade aerials on the roof used for communicating with aircraft

Above The bane of pilots for 25 years, the Raytheon MIM-23 HAWK SAM is used by frontline and reserve Marine Corps units. This rather lavishly camouflaged launch trailer and matching missiles belong to the 2nd Light Antiaircraft Missile Battalion, based at Yuma. The unit regularly spice up the training missions flown above the weapons ranges by deploying to the desert and acting as enemy SAM batteries

Right Another weapon guaranteed to bring tears to the eyes of grown pilots is the Stinger missile. Developed in the 1970s as a replacement for the M41 Redeye SAM, the Stinger system has proven itself to be virtually unbeatable in Afghanistan and Nicaragua. Only a one shot weapon, a single missile round is issued in a disposable launch tube requiring no maintenance or testing. This practice launcher uses the missile's infra-red seeker head to train potential users of the weapon

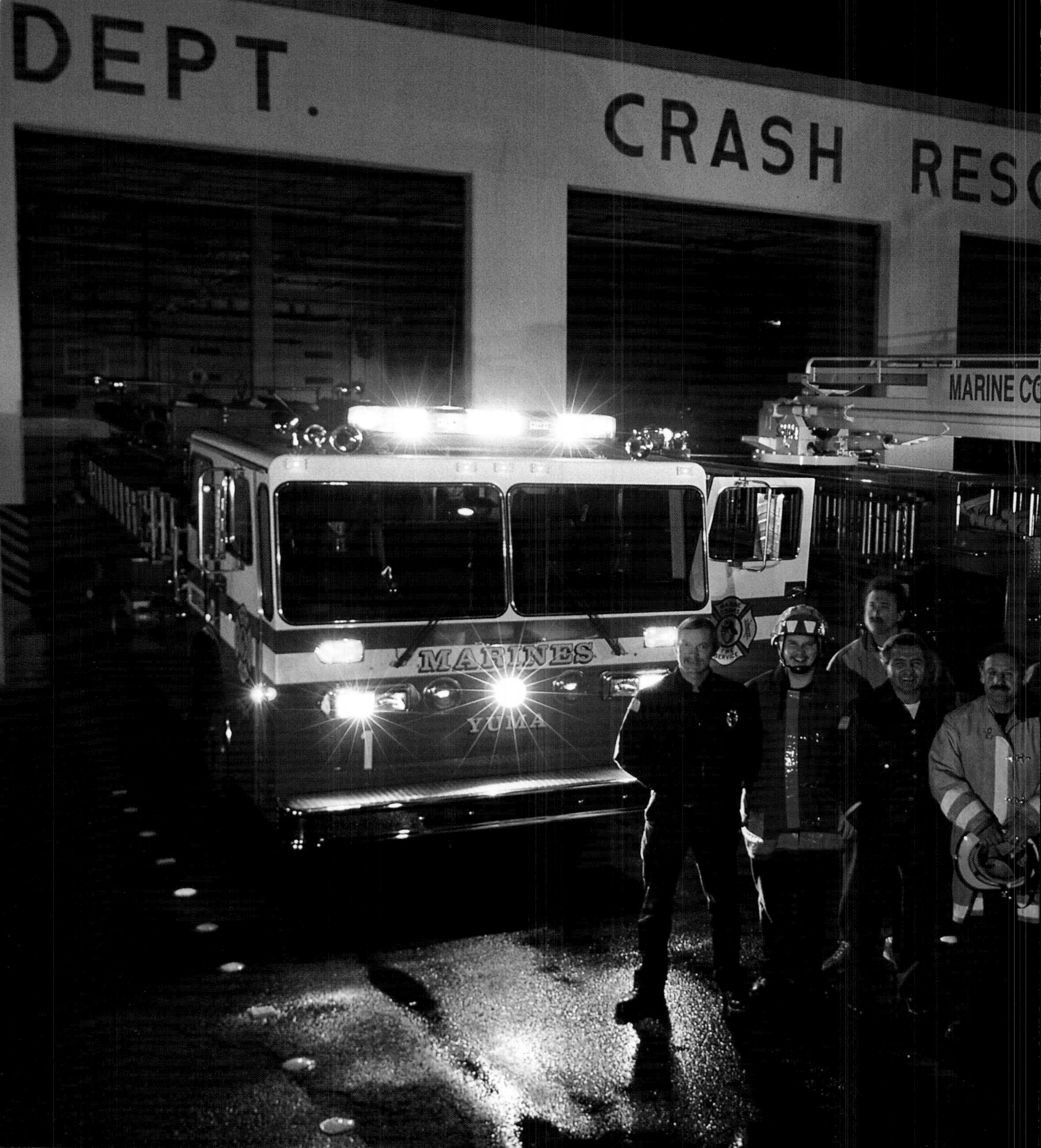
DEPT.
CRASH RESC
MARINE CO
MARINES
YUMA
1

Firefighter

Often taken for granted, but vital in the event of an accident, the crash crew form an integral part of the operational support at any air station or air base across the USA. Standing proudly outside the Yuma Fire Station, these Marine Corps firemen are just some of the highly trained professionals supporting Corps aviation in a less obvious, but no less important way

Above Just as in any other profession, practice makes perfect when you're a full time firefighter. Using a high pressure hose to combat a 'simulated' fuel fire, two suitably clad Marines work as a team to extinguish the JP-5 inferno

Left The heat at Yuma is unbearable at the best of times so heaven knows how a firefighter copes with it wearing a heavy, insulated protective suit. To help reflect radiation from the flames a transparently thin layer of pure gold is fitted to the hood's visor

Above Firefighters repose under a fiery Arizona sky

Heliborne

Left The ultimate in Marine Corps rotary muscle, an AH-1W Cobra sweeps over the fields and valleys *en route* to Yuma. Based at Camp Pendleton, the Whiskey model Cobra is flown by HMLA-169, the first attack helicopter squadron in the Corps to get their hands on the totally updated machine. Mounted on the stub wing is an AIM-9L Sidewinder and a seven-shot 2.75 inch rocket launcher. Bolted onto the stub wing above the ordnance is a small chaff launcher pack, although this one appears to be 'chaffless'

Below This starboard view of Cobra '132' reveals a totally different weapons suite to that which is fitted under the port wing stub. Mounted on the outboard pylon is a Hughes BGM-71 TOW (Tube-launched, Optically-tracked, Wire-guided) missile launcher, with a 19-shot 2.75 inch rocket pod alongside it

Above Charged with the responsibility of clearing a path through enemy positions to enable the transport elements of a helicopter assault force to land safely, the crews of HMLA-169 rely heavily on thorough training and a superb weapons platform to help them survive in arguably the most dangerous of combat roles. The new Cobra has an improved weapons suite, greater electronic countermeasures (ECM) capability and is powered by a pair of General Electric T700-GE-401 engines which drive larger chord blades

Right Assigned to HMLA-169, this UH-1N Huey is about to have a 7.62 mm Minigun fitted back into its purpose built mount before departing on a sortie. Attack helicopter squadrons usually have three or four Huey gunships operating alongside the dedicated attack Cobras

Left One role a Huey can perform that a Cobra can't is the pinpoint delivery of small squads of Marines. The twin engined UH-1N is used extensively by the Corps, more than 85 currently in frontline service. When an attack squadron deploys on cruise the usual composition of the unit is four to six Cobras together with a pair of Hueys

Above Besides the risky parachute delivery of Marines, rappelling is used extensively by the Corps, although the Huey must remain stationary while this is in progress, presenting itself as an easy target for enemy troops

Although the combat Hueys only stay at Yuma temporarily while on exercises, a rather more colourful UH-1N that spends all year round in the Arizona desert is the base rescue flight helicopter. Painted up in standard Navy rescue colours, this Huey mounts a powerful spotlight alongside the co-pilot's door. After completing yet another practice sortie out on the range, the crew return to the Yuma flightline surrounded by a breathtaking dusk sky

Left A more unusual visitor to the Yuma flightline is this SH-2F Seasprite from the fleet readiness squadron HSL-31 'Archangels'. As well as being an anti-submarine warfare helicopter, the Seasprite is often called upon to perform surface air rescue (SAR) work and this is where the extensive desert ranges of Yuma come in. Having returned from a SAR training mission, the US Navy pilot and Royal Navy exchange co-pilot discuss the results of the mission

Above The Marines always get their money's worth out of the combat types they operate, and one aircraft which proves this point perfectly is the venerable Boeing Vertol CH-46 Sea Knight. First flown over thirty years ago, the medium lift hauler has soldiered on as the Corps' rotary workhorse without any pomp or fanfare well past its originally expected retirement age. This CH-46E from HMM-163 is guided down onto terra firma by the loadmaster peering out of the crew door

Above Over the years the CH-46 has been progressively updated to keep it abreast of contemporary rotary trends. The Echo model has glassfibre rotor blades, uprated General Electric T58-16 engines of 1870 standard horsepower, crash attenuating crew seats, a combat resistant fuel system and improved rescue gear. Based at the huge MAG-16 helicopter facility at Tustin, California, a brace of CH-46E Sea Knights from HMM-163 zoom over the Yuma range at low level

Opposite above High over the desolate Arizona plains, a HMM-163 Sea Knight returns to Yuma after completing a troop drop. A total of 18 combat-ready Marines, or 4200 lb of cargo, can be carried by the Sea Knight at a maximum speed of 135 knots. The casing leading into the engine intakes has been retrofitted to all CH-46s in an effort to lower the heat signature of the helicopter to enemy SAMs. Bolt-on armour plating can also be seen around the engine housing

Opposite below Re-enacting a scene that could have taken place in the jungles of Vietnam, or on the beaches of Grenada, a CH-46 disgorges its troops under the watchful eyes of an unseen loadmaster toting an ancient .50 calibre machine gun which is mounted in the forward crew hatch. This Sea Knight belongs to HMM-161, one of five CH-46 squadrons based at MCAS Tustin

Opposite above A heavy lifter of gargantuan proportions, the Sikorsky CH-53E Super Stallion is the latest in the family of helicopters developed especially for the Marine Corps. Capable of carrying 55 combat-ready troops, the Super Stallion is powered by three General Electric T64-GE-416 turboshaft engines which boost its total power to 13,140 hp, more than doubling the original 5700 hp available to the twin engined CH-53D. This particular Stallion belongs to HMH-465 'Warhorses', based at MCAS Tustin

Opposite below Wearing an unusual white modex on the nose, a CH-53E from HMH-465 is marshalled in at Yuma by the helicopter's loadmaster. The massive rotors and hub are evident in this view, as is the retractable refuelling probe mounted beneath the cockpit floor

Left Suitably tough looking Marines pose in front of their multi coloured CH-53E from HMH-465. The 'Warhorses' are one of only three squadrons currently equipped with the Echo model Super Stallion

Overleaf The bond between 'rotary' Marines and 'mud' Marines is a strong one, a union that has been evolved through harsh combat in Korea, Vietnam and Grenada. Hiding amongst the saltbush, a squad awaits the imminent arrival of a flight of CH-53D Sea Stallions which will extract them from the harsh Arizona desert